Get Better Results!

Learn English Paragraph

*W*riting

Skills

Book I in the series "Academic Writing Skills"

ESL
Paragraph Essentials
for
International Students

Stephen E. Dew

Learn English Paragraph Writing Skills:

ESL Paragraph Essentials for International Students

(An ESL Paragraph Writing Skills Handbook for International Students)

Discover Academic Writing Skills

Visit Stephen E. Dew Amazon author page @ amazon.com/author/stephendew

Table of Contents

Preface

After receiving some feedback about my first book, "*Learn English Paragraph Writing Skills: ESL Paragraph Essentials for International Students*", released in May 2013, I decided to release a new and improved edition II.

Some of the feedback I received from my ESL students included:

- The tables are not easy to read or well formatted.
- The cover is not very interesting or exciting.
- The writing process could be expanded.
- Formatting could be improved.
- Some errors were also evident.

So what's Changed?

To provide the best possible experience for my ESL students, I have released edition II with:

- Images for some tables that have been inserted into an appendix.
- Some images have been set up as down-loadable for students to use.
- Additional images have been added for more clarity.
- A new and hopefully inspiring cover that people like.
- An expanded English writing process explaining more

practically "How to write a paragraph or essay."

- Improved formatting for each of the sections.
- Fixed issues with grammar, spelling, and missing words.

I am always open for feedback and will continue to improve and provide the best practical academic writing skills portable books for international ESL students.

Stephen E. Dew
Author of the Series
Academic Writing Skills

<u>Introduction</u>

Throughout my working career, I have noticed the need to make sure we write with understanding and clarity for our readers.

During my 30 years in the telecommunications industry, it was necessary for me to learn techniques associated to report writing, document writing, process writing, and writing for business strategy development. Of course, these aren't the only reasons to learn academic writing, but business and career reasons are by far a strong incentive to learn and understand good English writing techniques.

After I moved to Cambodia, in 2010, to teach English at well renowned university to undergraduates, I noticed a distinct lack of understanding of the English writing process, even-though, I had been told it was similar to English academic writing principles and guidelines. This could be due to a non-English speakers command of English, or it could be due to cultural norms or language differences, or maybe it's related to the way books try to explain ideas and concepts. I'm not really sure, however, it's probably a combination of these things and many more.

What I am sure of is a greater emphasis should be placed on academic writing skills when teaching English as a second language.

Most teaching books are written in a format that is sometimes above the level of understanding of non-English speakers, or perhaps not culturally relevant to their learning environment. They assume the ESL student is learning in the country they have migrated to. However, in Asian countries, the ESL student is learning English for a multitude of reasons; Not the least being to migrate.

One major reason is academic study, so it is necessary to ensure that non English speakers clearly understand the techniques for English academic writing in order for them to enter university with the required knowledge to succeed.

This book has been written with that in mind. The concept is to provide or supplement other learning materials in a condensed version to give ESL students a quick guide to the necessary English academic writing skills.

I have taught Academic writing to ESL students for over 3 years now and feel well qualified to provide the following reference material as quick guide to English academic writing.

The great thing about this book is ESL students around the world can carry it anywhere by using their android, apple, or kindle devices. I consider it a great resource to have when you need it!

What does this book offer you?

Well, look at the list of paragraph and English writing essentials I cover:

- Paragraph format
- Paragraph structure
- Paragraph organization
- Sentence structure
- Transition signals
- Capitalization
- Punctuation
- The academic writing process

I know you bought this book for a reason, and I'm pretty sure your reasons would be to:

- ✓ Improve your basic academic English writing knowledge and skills.
- ✓ Look much more adept and professional in your academic English writing.
- ✓ Show your classmates how easy academic English writing is.
- ✓ Finally impress your professor at university or in your regular English classes.
- ✓ Boost your self-confidence in English writing.
- ✓ Improve your grades.

You have made a wise purchase!

If you have a need to learn more about English academic writing skills then you have the right book.

I wish anyone who is reading and using this guide the best of luck in improving their English academic writing skills. However, In saying that, it's not up to luck so much as dedication, hard work, and an a personal interest in good English writing skills.

Notes

1. Although I have included some examples for clarity, I have intentionally left out practice exercises, as that is not the intention of this guide. International ESL students get plenty of practice in their regular classes, so this was written to supplement those classes with easy to read reference material.

2. If you are looking for some practice exercises, try *"English Writing Exercises for International Students: An ESL Grammar Workbook for ESL Essay Writing."* This is an Interactive Workbook written to support all my books in the series *"Academic Writing Skills"*. It can be found on Amazon at: *http://www.amazon.com/English-Writing-Exercises-International-Students-ebook/dp/B00GPI3CQK*

I. <u>What is Academic Writing?</u>

There are many forms of writing such as creative writing, personal writing, or academic writing.

So what is the difference?

Well creative and personal writing are for things like stories, emails, and letters to family and friends. Both creative and personal writing are informal, so writers can use slang, contractions, abbreviations, and even incomplete sentences.

Academic writing is different. Academic writing is a formal style of writing used for high school, university, and business writing. In these cases, formal means you must follow specific guidelines and ensure you use complete sentences, organize them in a logical way, and you do not use slang or contracted language.

When studying academic writing, there are several kinds of paragraph structure that you need to learn such as:

1. Narrative Paragraphs

Narrative writing is story writing in order of events, as they happen. You use time order to organize your paragraphs.

Figure 1 - Narrative Writing

2. *Descriptive Paragraphs*

Descriptive writing appeals to the reader's sense of smell, look, feel, taste and/or sound. Descriptive writing describes an object, image, place, or person so well that the reader gets a clear picture in their mind of what you are describing. You use space order to organize your paragraph.

3. *Process Paragraphs*

Process paragraphs explain process. They explain how to do something or make something. This is why they are sometimes called "How to" paragraphs. You use listing or time order to organize your paragraph.

4. Comparison and Contrast Paragraphs

Comparison paragraphs describe two or more things that are similar. Contrast paragraphs describe differences. Of course, you can write about both similarities and differences in the same paragraph or essay. This type of paragraph or essay is used quite widely for academic writing.

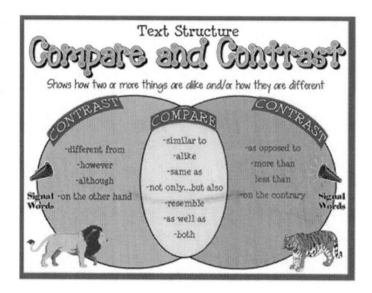

Figure 2 - Comparison and Contrast

5. Definition Paragraphs

Definition paragraph are used to define or explain something like a word or an idea, or you may need to explain an abstract concept. These are also used widely in Academic writing.

6. Opinion Paragraphs

Opinion paragraphs are important in academic studies.

Students, college graduates, and even business managers are asked every day to provide an opinion formally and support their opinion. This style of writing shows the reader what you think and why.

You should know what all of these styles are, but they are the topic of another discussion in the future, as I intend to follow this book with others in series of condensed academic writing guides for ESL students.

Note:

For now, we will focus on an electronic quick reference guide to supplement your ESL learning material.

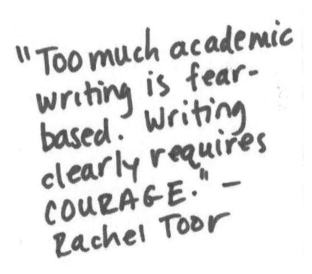

Figure 3 - Rachel Toor

II. <u>**Paragraph Format**</u>

Paragraph format is defined as the way you layout or write your words on paper, so to speak. Whether you use a computer or hand write your paragraph, you should follow these guidelines.

1. Your paper should be A4 (8.267 in x 11.692 in or 210 mm x 297 mm).
2. You should use black or blue ink when writing, and if typing, you should use a standard font such as Arial or Times New Roman without any mark up or emphasized text.
3. You must have a heading. A heading should provide your name, course number and due date.
4. You add your title in the center of the page after skipping a line from your heading. Ensure you underline your title.
5. Your sentences in the body of the paragraph should be double spaced, and the first sentence of a paragraph is indented about 1 in or 25 mm.
6. You leave a margin of about 1 in or 25 mm on the left and right side of your page. The bottom margin should also be about 1 in or 25 mm.

III. **Paragraph Structure**

A paragraph is a group of sentences discussing similar or related ideas of a topic.

In academic writing there are three parts to any paragraph.

1. The Topic Sentence
2. Supporting Sentences
3. The Concluding Sentence

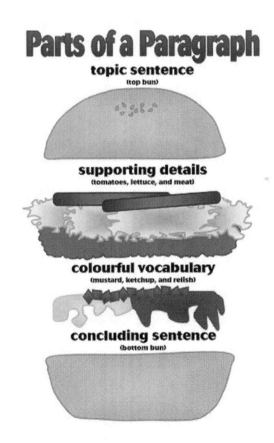

Parts of a Paragraph

topic sentence
(top bun)

supporting details
(tomatoes, lettuce, and meat)

colourful vocabulary
(mustard, ketchup, and relish)

concluding sentence
(bottom bun)

1. Topic Sentence

The topic sentence tells your reader the topic and the controlling idea of the paragraph. The topic is the subject being discussed. The controlling idea defines the scope or boundaries of the discussion. In other words, we will only discuss what the controlling idea says we will discuss.

Just as in the story of "Goldilocks and The Three Bears", topic sentences can be too broad, too specific, or just right! Developing a topic sentence is easy. You take the topic and brainstorm it for ideas. Then you take one of the sub-topics and brainstorm it again. One of these ideas can be used for your controlling idea.

2. Supporting Sentences

As an analogy, supporting sentences are the meat of a hamburger. They tell your reader the main ideas and supporting detail of the topic being discussed.

Developing supporting sentences is also relatively easy. You should turn the topic sentence into a topic question, and then answer the topic question. This will give you your main supporting detail.

For example:

Topic Sentence - "People give different reasons for skipping breakfast."

Topic Question - "What reasons do people give for skipping breakfast?"

Answers:

> They think it helps lose weight.
> They don't like breakfast.
> It could be cultural.
> No time.
> Too lazy.

3. Concluding Sentence

The concluding sentence tells your reader you have finished writing. You are not going to introduce any new ideas. When writing a concluding sentence, you can either restate the topic sentence in different words or summarize the main ideas being discussed.

IV. **Paragraph Organization**

In organizing your paragraph, you should provide some kind of logical order. This means you discuss each of your points or main ideas in a logical pattern within the paragraph.

For example, when using words like reasons, advantages, disadvantages, kinds, types, or qualities in your topic sentence, you should discuss each point separately in a logical order, point by point, within your paragraph.

As paragraphs are discussing related ideas, we make sure each sentence or idea connects to the next. To ensure paragraphs are well organized, use the 3 following concepts.

1. Paragraph Unity

Unity is a term used to describe "one idea - one paragraph". It means that all of your supporting sentences only discuss ideas directly related to the topic.

When writing English academically, is not acceptable to deviate from the main topic within a paragraph.

2. Paragraph Coherence

Paragraphs should follow the rule of coherence. A coherent paragraph runs like water, smoothly, from start to finish. Any reader can easily follow the ideas being presented because they are logically connected, and each sentence leads naturally to the next.

To achieve coherence in your paragraph follow these guidelines.

1. Use consistent nouns and pronouns in your paragraph. Don't mix them!
2. Use Transitional signals to show the relationship between sentence ideas.
3. Use logical order within your paragraph organization as discussed earlier

Let's look at each in more detail.

a. Consistent Pronouns

The use of consistent nouns and pronouns is one way to maintain paragraph coherence. It means if you start with the topic noun as singular, then all the pronouns and related nous of the topic noun should be singular.

Likewise, if you start with the topic noun as plural, then all the pronouns and nouns associated with the topic noun should be plural.

Note: If you are talking about groups of people, it is always best to write in plural.

b. Transition Signals

As paragraphs are discussing related ideas, we make sure each sentence or idea connects to the next. Transition signals show the relationship between sentences or paragraphs. To do this in English writing we use transitions signals.

As transition signals show the relationship between sentences, paragraphs will have connected related ideas within the paragraph.

The list below shows the different types of transition signals you should know; However, we will discuss them in more detail in the chapter on the English writing process.

- Sentence connectors
- Coordinating conjunctions
- Subordinates
- Others types including adjectives and preposition

Refer to appendix 1 for a list of transition signals and their functions.

c. Logical Order of Ideas

All your ideas within a paragraph must be presented in some kind of logical order. For example, time order, space order, or logical division organization. These are different ways to keep your paragraphs organized, logical, and easy to understand.

3. Sentence Openings

You might ask, "*Why would I vary my sentences openings in paragraphs?*" Well the answer is simple. It makes your essay more interesting, and shows that you understand what you are doing.

Put simply, it helps you look more professional when writing academic English.

When writing sentences, you vary the type of sentence, and the start of a sentence.

For example,

- Start a sentence with a prepositional phrase.
- Use appositives to give more meaning and definition to nouns.
- Alternatively, you can start with a dependent clause before the independent clause.

Furthermore, one other important point to remember is the type of transition signal used between paragraphs (of an essay) can also be varied to make things flow smoothly.

4. Parallel Structure

Finally, this note on parallel structure is for you to consider. When you write a sentence with a series of words or clauses, make sure that they start and end using the same form. If you don't, you will destroy the coherence you've tried to establish.

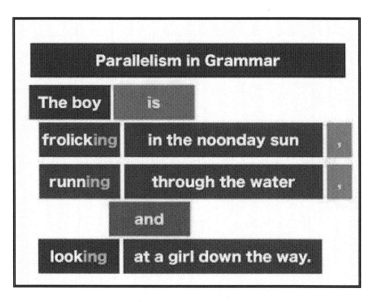

Figure 4 – Parallelism

More importantly, Robert M Knight said in an article I read, "*If you use parallel structures your readers will have a more enjoyable time absorbing and understanding your facts, ideas, and concepts.*" (Robert M. Knight, A Journalistic Approach to Good Writing. Wiley, (2003).

For example:

Jesse Jackson said, "Today's students can put dope in their veins or hope in their brains. If they can conceive it and believe it, they can achieve it. They must know it is not their aptitude but their attitude that will determine their altitude."

Notice the word forms are the same!

In summarizing paragraph organization, If you adopt these several concepts, you will look much more adept and professional, and I know that this is one of your goals for learning Academic English Writing.

Let your readers to enjoy, absorb, and understand what you have written, so use these guidelines for a better result. Write for your reader, not yourself.

Summary to Date

So now a quick reminder of what we have discussed so far. To date, we have discussed:

- ✓ What academic writing is?
- ✓ Why we use academic writing.
- ✓ Paragraph format and structure.
- ✓ Paragraph organization.

If you have not understood any of the above points then read them again.

If you wish to ask me any questions then leave a message on my contact page at my website.

http://hbicambodia.com/contact-the-author-stephen-e-dew.html

Next we are going to discuss:

- Capitalization
- Punctuation
- Sentence structure

Hopefully, they will be explained in a way that supplements

your understanding and perhaps help you to retain the knowledge even more.

v. <u>Capitalization</u>

In English, there are 4 basic rules for capitalization.

- The first word of sentence.
- The pronoun "I".
- Abbreviations and acronyms. *For instance*, UN.
- Proper nouns (a proper noun is a naming word).

The first 3 are easy to understand, however, proper nouns have many definitions in English. So you must be asking, "What defines a proper noun?" There are 10 rules that define proper nouns in English. You must simply learn them as you do mathematics.

Rule	Examples	Exceptions
Names of Deities (Gods)	God, Allah, Vishnu, Buddha	
Names of people and their titles	Mr. And Mrs. Stephen Dew, President Bush	Do not capitalize a title without a name
Names of specific groups of people (nationalities, languages, races, religions, and ethnic groups)	Cambodian, Khmer, Asian, Buddhist, Hispanic	
Names of specific places on a map	Phnom Penh, South Pole, Pacific Ocean, Railway Steet	
Names of specific geographic areas	Eastern Europe, Middle East	Do not capitalize compass directions, only locations
Names of days, months, and any special days	Friday, December, Easter, St. Valentines Day	Do not capitalize the seasons
Names of structures (buildings, bridges, dams, and monuments)	Buckingham Palace, Hoover Dam, Golden Gate Bridge, Nelsons Column	
Names of organisations (government departments, businesses, schools, and clubs)	National Treasury, Bank of New Zealand, National Australian University, Eagles Football Club	
Names of school subjects with course numbers	French 101, Human Biology 201, Chemistry 10A	Do not capitalize subjects without numbers, only Languages without numbers
Titles (books, magazines, movies, songs, statues, painting, newspapers, and TV programs)	New York Times, Angkor Thom Magazine, Star Wars, The Man from Snowy River	Note: italicize or underline books, magazines, newspapers, movies, and plays.

Figure 5 - Rules for Capitalization

VI. **Punctuation**

Punctuation is extremely important in English. It can mean the difference between being understood or misunderstood.

Figure 6 - Commas are Important!

In this section I have listed:

- 10 comma rules.
- 3 possessive rules.
- The rules for using quotations.

As I stated in the section on capitalization, you must simply learn these to be a successful academic English writer.

Did you see the difference in meaning in the image?

1. *Comma Rules*

The following List of comma rules are typical of what you need to learn and remember.

1. To separate items in a series of three or more things. Do not use commas for two things in a series.

For example: I make my bed, take a shower, and brush my teeth when I get up in the morning.

2. Before the coordinating conjunction in a compound sentence. Do not confuse a simple sentence with compound verbs or nouns with a compound sentence.

For example: I like to eat breakfast, and I like to read the newspaper before I go to school.

3. After a dependent clause that comes before an independent clause in a complex sentence.

For example: While I was eating dinner, the phone rang.

4. To separate additional or extra information in adjective clauses from the main sentence.

For example: I have been to Angkor Watt, which is in Cambodia.

5. To separate additional or extra information for appositives from the main sentence.

For example: Angkor Watt, the most famous temple in Cambodia, is near Siem Reap.

6. After most transition signals used at the start of a sentence. Don't use commas for then, now, and soon.

For example: However, Preah Vihear temple is more interesting.

7. To separate sentence connectors that join two independent clause.

For example: Angkor Watt is famous around the world, however, Prear Vihear temple is relatively unknown.

8. To separate day from month from year.

For example: Monday, 22nd April, 2013.

9. To separate street from suburb from city from country.

For example: #31 street 72, West Minister, Western Australia.

10. To separate 1000's in numbers.

For example: 1,000,000.

2. *Possessives (apostrophes)*

These are the possessive guidelines. Learn them as well!

- To replace missing letters in contractions.

For example: It is = it's.

- To show possession with nouns (and indefinite pronouns) for singular nouns and plural nouns which don't end in an "s".

For example: Child's room or Children's room.

- In plural nouns ending with "s".

For example: University students' meeting.

- To form plural numbers and letters.

For example: A plural = A's.

3. <u>Quotation Marks</u>

Quotation marks are used in academic English writing to separate the words someone else says or writes. You use this technique as a reported example to support your ideas or opinions. The basic guidelines for using quotations are as follows.

Use a reporting phrase such as:

- he said,
- he stated,
- he reported,
- according to

You can use "according to ..." when you want to name the person, magazine, or book you are getting the information from.

The reporting phrase can come before, in the middle, or at the end, but remember to separate the reporting phrase from the quotation using a comma. Also remember the verb tense can be any tense that is appropriate. Don't forget to capitalize the first word in the reported speech phrase.

For example: "One thing to do is to learn the rules for quotations", he said. He continued to say, "Also, learn the rules for commas."

When using a person or source that is not well known or credible, it is best to include the person's title or occupation in an appositive.

For example: Stephen Dew, an experienced TESOL instructor, said, "One thing to do is learn the rules for quotations."

You can see from the examples used the quotation marks (" ") are above the exact words stated.

If the reported phrase is long you can omit some words by placing [...] in the phrase. You can also add words, but they must be inside square brackets [ ].

For example: "One thing to do is learn the rules for commas ... the rules for quotation", he said.

For example: "One thing to do is learn the rules for commas [used in English]", he said.

If the reporting phrase comes at the end, periods, question marks, exclamations, and commas are inside the quotation marks.

Summary to Date

So now a quick reminder of what we have discussed so far. To date we have discussed:

- ✓ What academic writing is.

- ✓ Why we use academic writing.

- ✓ Paragraph format and structure.

- ✓ Paragraph organization.

- ✓ Capitalization

- ✓ Punctuation

If you have not understood any of the above points then read them again.

If you wish to ask me any questions then leave a message on my contact page at my website.

http://hbicambodia.com/contact-the-author-stephen-e-dew.html

Next we are going to discuss:

- Sentence structure

Hopefully, it will be explained in a way that supplements your understanding and perhaps help you to retain the knowledge even more.

VII. **Sentence Structure**

In English, there is never a sentence without a subject and verb.

Yes, I said, "and."

That means when you write a sentence it must have a subject and a verb. A sentence is an independent clause.

Sentence = Subject + Verb (+ complete thought)

In some languages, it may alright to drop a subject, however, in English this simply is not the case. If a sentence is missing either a subject or verb, it is a sentence error and must be fixed.

Even command sentences have a subject and verb. The subject may not be written, but it is implied.

For example: Open the door please!

In this sentence the subject is "you".

1. *Simple Sentences*

As stated earlier, a simple sentence is one Independent clause. A simple sentence has a subject and verb (and a complete thought). An independent clause is in fact a simple sentence. A kind of formula you can remember is an

Independent Clause = Simple Sentence.

A Simple sentence can also have a compound subject and / or a compound verb.

There are few types of simple sentences, but the follow four types are all you really need to get started.

Sentence Type	Example
SS = S + V	*My brother is a doctor.*
SS = S and S + V	*My brother and Sister are doctors.*
SS = S + V and V	*My father does not drink or smoke.*
SS = S and S + V and V	*My mother and father do not drink or smoke.*

Figure 7 - Sentence Types

SS   = Simple sentence
S   = Subject
V   = Verb

a. Subject Verb Agreement

Subject verb agreement states that the subject and verb in a sentence must agree in number. One way to remember this is a little saying I use, "single subject, single verb. plural subject, plural verb."

For example: My brother is a doctor. "My brother" is single subject; "is" is single verb.
For example: My brothers are doctors. "My brothers" is plural subject' "are" is plural verb.
For example: My brother and sister are doctors. "My brother and sister" is a plural subject; "are" is a plural verb.

Prepositional phrases can play a role in subject verb agreement, so here is a quick reminder of the definition of a prepositional phrase. A prepositional phrase consists of a preposition and a noun, pronoun, or noun phrase. Most prepositional phrases express time, place, and possession.

On most occasions, the prepositional phrase is ignored when determining subject verb agreement. However, as always, there are some exceptions.

The following tables will help you identify some subjects:

- that are always singular (regardless of the prepositional phrase).
- that are always plural (regardless of the prepositional phrase)
- that can be both singular or plural. (In these cases you look at the object of the preposition, in the prepositional phrase to decide the subject verb agreement.

b. Rules for Subject Verb Agreement

1. Singular Subjects:

The following words are always singular subjects even if plural in meaning.

		it	one	much
everyone	someone	anyone	no one	each
everybody	somebody	anybody	nobody	either
everything	something	anything	nothing	neither

For example: Everybody is here.

For example: Each of these phones is new.

For example: It is to help with your lessons.

- If using each or every before singular subjects joined by

an "and", a singular verb is used.

For example: Every woman and child is free to enter.

For example: Each worker and team leader has a desk.

- Words that come between a subject and verb do not change the number of the subject.

For example: The man along with his 2 children went for a walk.

- Titles of books and movies, even if plural in meaning or form always take a singular verb.

For example: Star Wars was great.

- There, here, and where are never subjects. When a sentence begins with one of these words, the subject comes after the verb.

For example: There are no problems writing an academic paragraph.

2. Plural Subjects:

Some subjects are plural and use a plural verb.

trousers	scissors	riches	several
jeans	tweezers	thanks	many

pants	pliers	means	both
			(a) few

For example: Both are going abroad.

For example: Only a few have failed the exam.

- Subjects joined by "and" or "both ...and" use a plural verb.

For example: Mum and dad are going abroad.

For example: Both mum and dad are going abroad.

- Some nouns are plural in form and always use a plural verb. However, if the noun follows expressions like "a pair of ..." or other expressions like "a word of ..." then the verb is singular.

For example: Her jeans are still dirty. (Plural)

For example: That pair of jeans is torn. (Singular)

3. Both Singular or Plural Subjects

Many words are singular or plural depending on what the refer to. When these words are followed by a prepositional phrase, the object of the preposition is used to determine the subject is singular or plural.

none
all
some
any
most
majority
half

For example: Some (of the ice) is melted. (Single)

For example: Some (of the ice cubes) are melted. (Plural)

- When subjects are joined by the following structures, the verb must agree with the closest subject.

neither ... nor...
either ... or ...
not only ... but also ...

For example: Neither the teachers nor the students are allowed to leave until the exam is finished.

For example: Not only the police officers, but also the police commander is coming.

- The expression "a number of" is plural, and the expression "the number of is singular".

For example: A number of students were missing from class.
For example: The number student in class was low.

- Expressions of time, money, weight, and volume are plural expressions, but they use a singular verb.

For example: Two thousand dollars a month is a good salary in Cambodia.
For example: Two weeks' vacation is not enough time to travel Cambodia.

- Some words are plural in form but singular in meaning. These words use a singular verb. Subject Verb Agreement for Subjects, Diseases, and Abstract Nouns are some of these words. See the table for some examples.

Subjects	Diseases	Abstract nouns
mathematics	measles	news
economics	mumps	politics

Subjects	Diseases	Abstract nouns
statistics	herpes	ethics

For example: Physics is an easy subject.

For example: The news wasn't very good.

- Collective nouns are usually singular, but they can be plural depending on the pronoun.

class
police
family
team
audience
committee
faculty

For example: That class had its exam on Friday. (its - singular)

For example: The class were working on their writing assignment. (their - plural)

- Some nouns have the same form for singular or plural. Words like species, deer, sheep, and series have the same form for singular and plural. So watch the pronouns again for these words.

For example: That species is very rare. (singular pronoun)
For example: Those species are very common. (plural pronoun)

- Some nouns for nationality can be singular or plural. Words like Chinese, English, and French can be singular or plural. When a word refers to a language, it uses a singular verb. When the word refers to the people in a country, it uses a plural verb and has the article "the" in front of it.

For example: English is an international language. (language - singular)
For example: The English are very conservative. (people - plural)

- Words from other languages that English has borrowed can have very unusual singular and plural forms.

Origin	Singular	Plural	Example
Greek	-is	-es	crisis / crises

Origin	Singular	Plural	Example
Greek	-on	-a	criterion / criteria
Latin	-us	-i	radius / radii
Latin	-um	-a	medium / media
Latin	-ix / -ex	-ices	appendix / appendices

For example: The radius of the circle is two meters.

For example: The criteria are difficult to meet.

2. *Compound Sentences*

A compound sentence is two or more simple sentences (remember a simple sentence is an Independent clause) connected by a comma and a coordinating conjunction.

Do not to confuse a simple sentence that has a compound subject or verb with a compound sentence.

A compound sentence is two independent clauses (IC) joined by a comma and coordinating conjunction. We remember the coordinating conjunctions by using an acronym "FANBOYS".

F - for

A - and

N - nor

B - but

O - or

Y - yet

S - so

A good formula to remember for a compound sentence is:

IC +, coordinating conjunction + IC.

For Example: I like writing, so I write books.

Coordinating Conjunctions

Coordinating conjunction	Use	Example
and	Joins sentences that are alike or add another idea.	I like to drink coffee, and I like to drink tea.
or	Joins sentences that give you choice.	You can have coffee, or you can have tea.
but	Joins sentences that are opposite or add an opposing idea.	I like to write, but i don't get much chance.

Coordinating conjunction	Use	Example
so	Joins sentences where the second sentence is a result of the first.	I like to write, so I write books.
for	Similar meaning to because. We use for when want to introduce a reason or cause for something.	I like to write, for I am good at it. (I like to write because I'm good at it.)
yet	Similar meaning to "but". Use yet when the second IC shows something unexpected with respect to the first IC.	I was running late for class, yet I didn't seem to care too much.

Coordinating conjunction	Use	Example
nor *	Nor means is not this and not that. Nor joins two negative sentences.	I haven't gone home yet, nor have I eaten dinner.

Figure 8 - Coordinating Conjunctions

Note 1: When using "nor", the word order is important. Notice, "nor have I eaten dinner." After the comma nor, we use an auxiliary verb and then the subject. See how it appears like a question after nor! It's not a question, but the word order appears like a question.

3. *Complex Sentences*

A complex sentence is a combination of one Independent clause (IC) and one or more dependent clauses (DC).

So you know what an independent clause is, but what is a dependent clause?

As quoted by Wikipedia, "A dependent clause (or a subordinate clause) is a clause that augments an independent clause with additional information, but which cannot stand alone as a sentence. Dependent clauses either modify the independent clause of a sentence or serve as a component of it. Some grammarians use the term subordinate clause as a synonym for dependent clause. Other grammars use subordinate clause to refer only to adverbial dependent clauses. There are also different types of dependent clauses, including noun clauses, relative (adjectival) clauses, and adverbial clauses."

That's a real mouthful, but for our purposes, a dependent clause = a subordinating conjunction + IC. Therefore, subordinates always come at the beginning of a dependent clause. A dependent clause depends on and Independent clause to complete it's meaning. It is not a sentence, so it can't stand alone as a sentence. It is a sentence error if it is not connected to an independent clause.

a. Subordinating Conjunctions

Subordinating conjunctions or subordinates are broken down into:

- Time
- Reason
- Place
- Contrast

Subordinates of Time	Example
after	She goes to work after she finishes school.
as	The parade passed as they stood and watched.
as soon as	She went to the teacher's room as soon as she got to school.
before	You have to take a test before you study English.
since	It has been 3 years since I left Australia.
until	We won't start until everyone has arrived.
when	When you study English, you have to study hard.
whenever	I feel tired whenever I don't sleep well.
while	The parade passed while they stood and watched.

Subordinates of Reason	Example

Subordinates of Reason	Example
because	*She gets high grades because she studies hard.*
as	*As she wants to pass her exam, she studies very hard.*
since	*Since she studies hard, she should pass her exam.*

Subordinates of Place	Example
where	*I can never remember where I put my reading glasses.*
wherever	*I take my reading glasses wherever I go.*

Subordinates of Contrast	Example
although	*My sister still loves me although we disagree about mum and dad.*

Subordinates of Contrast	Example
even though	*My sister still loves me even though we disagree about mum and dad.*
though	*My sister still loves me though we disagree about mum.*
while *	*I think mum should sell the house, while my sister doesn't.*
whereas *	*I think mum should sell the house, whereas she doesn't.*

* Note: When using "while" and "whereas", use a comma even if the independent clause comes first.

b. Appositives

A good writer develops an ability to use appositives. It is the sign of a mature writer.

Appositives are nouns or noun phrases that refer to the preceding noun. So, an appositive is a noun or noun phrase that tells us more about the noun before it. Appositives can give us extra information about a noun without having to write verbose definitions. They are good for descriptive writing.

Appositives can be non-defining or defining.

Non-defining Appositives

Non-defining appositive clauses give extra information about the noun, but they are not essential or necessary. The preceding noun is enough to identify who or what you are talking about. The noun can be identified as one of kind.

Appositives of one of kind are always non-defining. Words that are superlatives like oldest, youngest, tallest, highest, and noun clauses like the language of Cambodia are all one of a kind and do not need extra information to identify them any further.

For these kinds of words there is no other to identify. There can only be one, therefore, it is identified.

Note, when using non-defining appositives, we use commas to separate the appositive from the main sentence.

For example: Khmer, the language spoken by Cambodian people, is difficult to learn.
For example: My youngest son, William, is an Australian citizen.

Defining Appositives

Defining clauses give necessary information about the noun in order to identify it more specifically to one of a kind.

For example: My son William is an Australian citizen.

In this example, William is the appositive, and it refers to the noun son. The appositive William is necessary to identify which son is an Australian citizen.

c. Adjective Clauses

An adjective clause is a dependent clause used as an adjective within a sentence. Adjective clauses usual define people, things, or time. They are also known as a relative clause.

An adjective clause (or relative clause) usually begins with a relative subject pronoun (which, that, who, whom, whose), a relative object pronoun (where, when, why), or no relative pronoun at all.

Pro noun	People / Things	Subject / Object	Necessary / unnecessary
who	people	subject	both
whom	people	object	both

Pro noun	People / Things	Subject / Object	Necessary / unnecessary
which	animals or things	both	extra only
that	animals or things	subject or object	necessary only
when	time		both

Pro Noun	Example
who	My brother, who is a doctor, lives in Cambodia.
whom	*He gave his keys to someone whom he did not know.* *He gave his keys to the headmaster, whom he has known for three years.*

Pro Noun	Example
which	*He teaches us academic writing, which I enjoy very much.*
that	*The group that meets here each weeknight is an academic writing class.* *The subject that I enjoy the most is academic writing.* *The subject I enjoy the most is academic writing.*
when	*I study academic writing when I have free time.* *I didn't study academic writing last week, when I had my exam.*

The two main kinds of adjective clauses are defining or non-defining adjective clauses.

Non-defining Adjective Clauses.

For example: The biggest black dog, which has no tail, is a Doberman.

As with appositives, we don't need the extra information in

order to understand the sentence. Note that non-defining adjective clauses are usually separated by commas, and "that" is not usually used in this kind of non-defining adjective clause.

Defining Adjective Clauses

For example: The dog that has no tail is a Doberman.

We need the adjective clause "that has no tail" in order to understand the sentence. Without the relative clause, we don't know which dog is being referred to.

Note: "that" is often used in defining relative clauses, and they are not separated by commas as with non-defining adjective clauses.

For example: People who come late will not be able to join us.

4. Noun Clauses

A noun clause is a dependent clause that functions as a noun (that is, as a subject, object, or complement) within a sentence, but it cannot stand as a sentence.

A noun clauses can begin with a 'wh' question word, whether or if, and that. These are common ways to express noun clauses.

For example: What you do doesn't really matter.

For example: I don't know what she does.

5. Adverb Clauses

An adverb clause has a subject and verb as do all clauses. It functions as an adverb. You will find a subordinate conjunction at the start of an adverb clause. This keeps the clause from expressing a complete thought. An adverb clause answers one of these three adverb questions: How? When? or Why?

For example: I read the book until my eyes ached.

Complex Sentence Summary

A complex sentence is a combination of one Independent clause (IC) and one or more dependent clauses (DC).

A good formula to remember what a complex sentence is:

Complex sentence = IC + DC
or
Complex sentence = DC, + IC.

Notice the comma when the dependent clause comes first.

Earlier we discovered what a dependent clause was, and we also saw some subordinates we use. In particular time, reason, or place. Remember a dependent clause is a subordinate + IC, and it is not a sentence, so it can't stand alone as a sentence. If it is not connected to an independent clause, it is a sentence error.

VIII. <u>Types of Sentence Errors</u>

1. Fragments

The word fragment means a part or piece of something. Put simply, fragments are a sentence missing a part. Fragments can be missing a subject or a verb. If a sentence is missing a subject or verb, that makes it a fragment. Fragments are sentence errors and must be fixed by adding either a subject or verb.

For example: Will go shopping tomorrow. (Missing a subject)
For example: I will go shopping tomorrow.

For example: I will go shopping tomorrow. (Missing a verb)
For example: I will go shopping tomorrow.

2. Run On

A Run on is also sentence error. They occur when 2 independent clause are joined together incorrectly.

For example: Men watch football women go shopping.

This example is a run on. There are actually 2 independent clauses.

1. Men watch football.
2. Women go shopping.

The sentence error should be fixed by either inserting a period and capital letter for women, or making a compound sentence from the 2 independent clauses.

For example: "Men watch football. Women go shopping." or "Men watch football, but women go shopping."

There is third way to fix these sentence errors. When you become more proficient with sentence connectors you could have used "Men watch football, however, women go shopping."

3. Comma Splice

Comma splices are also sentence errors. They occur when you join 2 independent clauses with a comma.

For example: Men watch football, women go shopping.

This is a Comma splice. There are actually 2 independent clauses here.

   a. Men watch football.
   b. Women go shopping.

The sentence error should be fixed by either inserting a period and capital letter for women, or making a compound sentence from the 2 independent clauses.

For example: "Men watch football. Women go shopping. or

Men watch football, but women go shopping."

There is third way to fix these sentence errors. When you become more proficient with sentence connectors you could have used "Men watch football, however, women go shopping."

Summary to Date

So now a quick reminder of what we have discussed so far.
To date we have discussed:

- ✓ What academic writing is.

- ✓ Why we use academic writing.

- ✓ Paragraph format and structure.

- ✓ Paragraph organization.

- ✓ Capitalization

- ✓ Punctuation

- ✓ Sentence structure

If you have not understood any of the above points then read
them again.

If you wish to ask me any questions then leave a message on my contact page at my website.

http://hbicambodia.com/contact-the-author-stephen-e-dew.html

Next we are going to discuss the English Writing Process in more detail. Hopefully, it will be explained in a way that supplements your understanding and perhaps help you to retain the knowledge even more.

IX. The English Writing Process Overview

You might asking, "Why do I need to follow an writing process?" Well the simple answer is you become a more effective and efficient writer. The writing process establishes the discipline to become a good academic English writer. One who produces outstanding paragraphs or essays each and every time.

The writing process is a simple and easy to follow technique which improves your academic writing skills, and hence, improves your results. As you can see, the writing process has 5 main steps with the 5th being the final copy you submit to your tutor, instructor, or professor.

The 5 Step Essay Writing Process

Follow the academic essay writing process if you want to write a good English academic paragraph or essay! You must *practice and apply each of the 5 steps* if you want better grades.

Pre-write

Pre-writing is the first step you use. Pre-writing helps you to get ideas on a topic. In this step, you write down your ideas in any way or form that helps you remember them. There several techniques for pre-writing which we will discuss latter.

Organize

Most students tend to understand outlining, but they fail to understand that outlining is actually a part of the organizing step. Organizing allows you to group your ideas and provide some logical order to your writing. When you organize your pre-writing you follow these two sub steps.

- Look at your list of ideas and group them logically. Circle ideas you want to use. Delete ideas you believe are unnecessary or duplicated.
- Once this part is completed, you do an outline.

An outline helps you organize or arrange your ideas in a logical order. It's like building a house. First, lay the foundations, then build the walls, and finally add the roof.

Outlines can be simple or detailed. We will discuss outlines in more detail in the section on organization.

Write your first draft

Here you follow your outline to write your draft essay. Write it as quickly as possible, and don't worry about too many mistakes. It's OK to make some mistakes because it is only a draft. You will fix any errors in step 4.

Review and Edit

As with everything we do in life, we check and review our actions. The same applies to your writing. We normally do two kinds of reviews for our writing. The first is a peer review, and the second is a self edit.

Final copy

Once you have your feedback from your peer review and completed your self-edit, you should write your final polished version using the English academic writing skills you have learned from our handbook.

X. **Detailed English Writing Process**

Step 1 -Pre-Write

There are a number of techniques or kinds of pre-writing that you should learn. Here are the 5 most common ways of pre-writing used by ESL students.

a. Note Taking

With this pre-writing technique, you usually do some kind of interview or research to get information about your topic. You take notes on the information given or found.

b. Free Writing

Free writing is a technique where you start to write and continue writing without stopping until you reach your desired topic. In this technique, sentence structure, spelling, and grammar do not matter. The main aim is to keep writing, and not to stop until you reach your topic idea that you wish to write about.

c. Listing

Listing is another technique which is really divided into two parts. In the first part, you make general ideas about the topic you have been given. In the second part, you choose one of the ideas and make a more detailed list about the topic you chose.

Figure 9 – Brainstorm

d. Brain Storming

The brainstorming technique only has one rule. You should set a time limit when brainstorming. Brainstorming is similar to listing. You start by writing the topic at the top of the page, and then you write your ideas down in list on your paper. Make sure you write everything done. Just keep writing ideas down in words or short phrases, and it doesn't matter about any mistakes you make. You can change or delete ideas latter in the writing process.

e. Clustering

This technique uses circles on paper with connected ideas. You begin clustering by drawing a circle in the middle of your page and write the topic inside. When you think of related ideas, you write these ideas in circles around the topic circle.

Each related idea in turn produces more related ideas. Once you have finished you can easily see where most of your rich ideas are. The rich ideas become the basis for your paragraph. Clustering offers the further advantage of grouping your ideas logically.

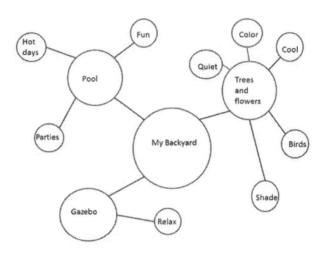

Figure 10 - Cluster Diagram

These are all different techniques or ways to pre-write to get ideas about your topic. Which one is best? Well that's up to you, but in my experience, brainstorming and clustering are the preferred methods used by most ESL students before they begin to write an academic paper.

Step 2 – Outline

Most students tend to understand outlining, but they fail to recognize that doing an outline is actually a part of the organizing step. When you organize your pre-writing you follow these two sub steps.

- First, you look at your list (or cluster) and group your ideas logically. Circle ideas you want to use. Delete ideas you believe are unnecessary or duplicated. Sometimes your ideas may be better organized into a table with category headings, so that you can use the categories for your main ideas.
- Once this part is completed, you do an outline. An outline helps you organize or arrange your ideas in a logical order. As I said, It's like building a house. First, you lay the foundations. Then you build the walls. Finally you add the roof.

Outlines can be simple or detailed. When writing a paragraph, a simple outline is fine, however, when writing an essay, I suggest you use a detailed outline.

Referring to the figure below, the number of main supporting points can be more or less, and the amount of supporting detail can be more or less. It all depends on you, and how much you need to write. You may have no supporting detail for a particular main idea, or you may have five or six supporting sentences.

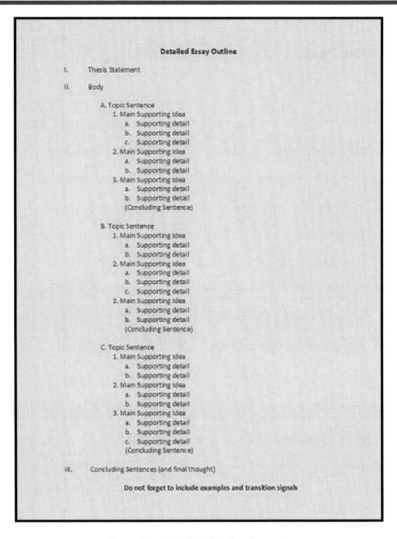

Figure 11 - Detailed Outline Example

When writing your outline include your paragraph transition signals and your supporting evidence. For instance, your examples, quotes, or facts or statistics you have found. Including this detail, at this stage of the academic writing process, will help when it comes to putting pen to paper in the next step.

Step 3 - First Draft

Don't get it right, just get it written.

James Thurber

After you have done your pre-writing and outline, you are ready to start writing your first draft. One misconception that some students have is they think the first draft is the finished product. However, the first draft is only step 3 of the English writing process.

The main idea of the first draft is to get the ideas down on paper, and to get your content the way you want it. In fact, I sometimes write a couple of drafts to get my paragraphs and essays the way I want. It all depends on how well you develop your ideas in the first two steps.

Once I've finished my first draft, I take a small break for a couple of hours. By taking a break, after I come back, I have a clear mind, and I take a fresh look at what I've written.

In essay writing, a lot of students just don't know where to start with an introduction, so if you are one of those people, skip the first paragraph (the introduction) and start with the body paragraphs. You can go back and write the introductory paragraph after you have completed the other paragraphs.

Likewise, you can skip any of the paragraphs when you are writing your first draft. The point I am trying to make is keep writing and go back latter to work on finishing your first draft.

The main idea is to keep writing as it is important not to interrupt the flow of words and ideas. During this step, do not spend time revising anything. It doesn't matter if you make any mistakes with spelling, grammar, or sentence structure. After all it is only a draft. You will fix any problems you have in step 4, peer-edit and self-review.

So, to get started, have your outline, your notes, your examples and citations available. If you have done your outline properly, you can draft the paragraph or essay in one sitting. Get yourself into the flow of writing, and don't worry about any errors because your words will flow more easily. This helps you find the connections between the main ideas. Don't rush, but try to get the essay from your head onto the page.

The tips I have outlined above can be used for any paragraph or essay, but at some stage you will have to write a more complex or longer essay.

Think of how your long, complex paper would look if it were

broken into smaller related assignments. Think of what it would look like and how it would read. What would the main parts be? Compare the main parts to the outline that you have already created.

Each piece of the smaller parts will, of course, be expanded in the longer academic assignment. However, by thinking of it in this way, you can work on each part with the idea of what you're trying to accomplish with each individual piece, but you will also have a good idea of how all the parts will fit together to form the whole essay.

In these cases, I have the following few suggestions.

- Make sure your outline is well prepared and detailed.
- Leave the introduction and conclusion until last.
- Chunk your writing times. That means write your essay in smaller parts. I usually write by paragraph. I treat each paragraph as a separate piece of my work. Don't try to write the whole essay in one sitting, instead, have a small break between each chunk you write.
- Always use your notes and outline. Use them for each paragraph you write, but remember to write each paragraph in separate sittings.
- Once you have finished all of the paragraphs, write your introductory paragraph, and when that is finished, read the whole essay, and then write your concluding

paragraph.

Yes, your essay may seem disjointed after the first draft, but that's O.K! In the revise and edit stage, you can work on transition signals, examples, citations, and on making the paper feel whole and connected.

Step 4 - Revise and Edit

As with everything we do in life, we check and review our actions. It comes from a continuous improvement cycle, PDCA, which means plan, do, check, and act. The same applies to your academic English writing.

By the time you get to step 4, you have completed the "PLAN" and "DO" stage, and now you are into the "CHECK" phase.

We normally do two kinds of reviews or checks for our academic English writing.

a. Peer Review

A peer review means a peer reviewer should read your essay, ask questions about it, and they should make some comments on what they think is good, or what they think should be changed to make your essay more clear.

When selecting a peer reviewer, look for someone such as a respected classmate, an instructor, a parent, or perhaps even a mentor you may have. It must be someone who is impartial and prepared to give you quality constructive feedback, and someone whose knowledge and skills you value and respect.

The idea is the peer reviewer should help improve your content and organization, so they do not check for grammar, punctuation, or spelling.

The peer review itself should be an interactive dialogue between you and the peer reviewer.

Remember the peer reviewer is there to help you. You selected them because you value their feedback, so don't take their comments the wrong way. Learn from their feedback, and you will become a more professional English writer. In fact, the more you listen and use their comments, the better your next written paragraph or essay, thus, you should expect less feedback each time as you improve your academic writing skills.

The peer reviewer should check for things like:

- Is the topic clear?
- Was the paragraph interesting?
- Did the reviewer learn anything?
- Did they understand everything?
- Do they need more information?
- Should something be included in the paragraph?
- Should something be removed from the paragraph?

- Is the paragraph on topic?
- Is the paragraph coherent?

Peer Review Checklist

Title: _____

Reviewer: _____

Comments:

Is the topic clear?

_____

Were the paragraphs interesting?

_____

Did you learn anything?

_____

Did you understand everything?

_____

Do you need more information?

_____

Should something be included in the paragraph?

_____

Should something be removed from the paragraph?

_____

Is the paragraph on topic?

_____

Is the paragraph coherent?

_____

Does the conclusion summarize or restate the topic sentence in different words?

_____

What did you like about the essay?

_____

all rights reserved hokamsoda@ 2013

Figure 12 - Peer Review Checklist

- Does the conclusion summarize or restate the topic

sentence in different words?

b. Self-Edit

A self-edit means you check your first draft for any errors. It's like polishing your car. You make sure your academic writing is an interesting, polished piece of work for others to read.

When you do your self-check you should check for things like:

1. Title
- Is the title appropriate?
- Have I use the rules of titles?
- Essay and Paragraph Format
- Is my essay and paragraph format correct?
2. Essay and Paragraph Organization and Structure
- Does my essay address the topic?
- Do my paragraphs have a good topic sentence and concluding sentence?
- Do my transition signals connect my ideas correctly?
- Do my paragraph transition signals connect my paragraphs?
- Do my examples to support my ideas?
- Does my paragraph follow the rules of unity and coherence?
3. Grammar and Sentence Structure.
- Do I have any sentence errors?

- Have I used a combination of sentence types like simple sentences, compound sentences, and complex sentences?
- Have I varied sentence openings by using some prepositional phrases or independent clauses?

4. Punctuation and Capitalization

- Have I used a period, question mark, or exclamation mark at the end of each sentence?
- Have I used commas according to the commas rules and sentence structure?
- Have I used capitals correctly?
- Is my spelling correct?
- Have I used reported speech correctly?

5. And finally, you should also check or add any cited sources that you have used for your supporting evidence.

Self-Edit Checklist

Title: _____

Sentences

- ☐ Do all sentences focus on one thought?
- ☐ Do I have any sentence errors (fragments, comma splices, or run ons)?
- ☐ Have I used a combination of sentence types like simple sentence, compound sentences, and complex sentences?
- ☐ Do sentences vary in length?
- ☐ Have I varied sentence openings by using some prepositional phrases or dependent clauses?

Paragraphs

- ☐ Does each paragraph focus on one idea or topic (unity)?
- ☐ Does each paragraph have a topic sentence, sentences with supporting details, and a concluding sentence?
- ☐ Are paragraph transitional signals been used where appropriate?
- ☐ Have I included examples?
- ☐ Do all paragraphs have the correct punctuation?

Spelling

- ☐ Is my spelling correct and I have checked with a dictionary?
- ☐ Did I use a thesaurus to vary my word choices?

Grammar

- ☐ I have used the correct subject verb agreement.
- ☐ I have used the correct pronouns.
- ☐ I have used the tenses correctly.
- ☐ Have I used a period, question mark, or exclamation mark at the end of each sentence?
- ☐ Have I used a period, question mark, or exclamation mark at the end of each sentence?
- ☐ Have I used capitals correctly?
- ☐ Am I using reported speech correctly, and is punctuation correct?

Overall

- ☐ Paragraphs are in the correct order.
- ☐ Point of view is clear and focused.
- ☐ Citation is included.

Figure 13 - Self-edit Checklist

Step 5 - The Final Copy

The final copy is what you will hand in to your professor or instructor as the completed paragraph or essay.

Through the review and edit step, all the poor sentences, incorrect transition signals between paragraphs, grammar and spelling errors of a first draft will disappear slowly before your eyes. Moreover, use the feedback and comments from your peer reviewer. If you use the feedback, your academic writing will again look more accomplished.

Ensure you follow all the rules of paragraph format and organization to write your final draft. Make sure you leave plenty of time to write your polished version. This helps the final product look more accomplished, formal, and professional.

Start writing!

Before you give your polished final draft to your professor or Instructor, read what you have written at least once more. You may find something wrong with your paragraph or essay at the last minute. If you do, fix it before you hand it in.

If your polished essay has too many corrections, it obviously needs another review.

For a final evaluation, you should decide if your essay fits the writing assignment, and does it achieved the assignment goals.

Use this checklist for your final draft before you hand it in.

1. Content:

   - Is the assignment complete?
   - Is the information appropriate?

2. Organization:

   - Is the order of the information logical?
   - Are the introduction and conclusion clear and related?

3. Style:

   - Are the style and tone appropriate?
   - Are the sentences smooth and efficient?
   - Is the diction appropriate, concrete, and accurate?
   - Is the paper free from mechanical errors?

4. Format:

- Is the assignment in the required format?

When answer a sound yes to all of these questions your final polished essay is ready to hand in.

Assignment Finished

Summary

Well it's that simple!

I'm just kidding. Even though I said simple, I really mean that it's not difficult if you follow the writing process. Sure it takes time and effort, but consider the *rewards* of learning English Academic Writing.

Combine your learning a with the writing process and you will become a proficient academic writer in no time. I also said *rewards*, because as an effective and efficient writer the sky is the limit.

In other words you can write your way to a BA.

You should put this book on your personal electronic devices. If you do, you can carry the information with you, and you will be able to use it as a quick English writing reference whenever you need it. You can also use it to supplement your regular English writing tutorials in class.

This is what we covered:

- Paragraph format
- Paragraph structure
- Paragraph organization
- Transition signals
- Capitalization
- Punctuation
- Sentence structure

- The academic writing process

In conclusion, at the start of this book, we looked at your reasons for buying this book. Besides writing your way to a BA, these are your *rewards*.

Let's do a recap of those *rewards*:

- Improve your basic writing knowledge and skills.
- Look much more adept and professional in your academic English writing.
- Show your classmates how easy English academic writing really is.
- Finally, impress your professor at university or in your regular English class.
- Boost your self-confidence in English academic writing.
- And not the least being **improved** grades.

With this book, you will achieve your goals and get your rewards, but only If you are prepared to **practice** writing and stick to the writing process until it is a part of your academic writing skill set, and **apply** your newly learned knowledge with the practical writing skills you have learned.

You are now fully equipped to write an excellent paragraph, essay, assignment, article, or thesis for that matter for your university course. I sincerely wish you good luck in your academic studies, and truly hope you found this ebook valuable now, and in the future as good reference material for your academic writing skills.

If you wish to ask me any questions, please leave a message on my contact page at my website.

http://hbicambodia.com/contact-the-author-stephen-e-dew.html

If you enjoyed or learned something from this book, I would appreciate if you could leave a review on *Amazon*.

About the Author: Stephen E. Dew

Figure 14 - The Author

The author, Stephen E. Dew, is a veteran of 33 years in the Telecommunication Industry from Australia. He obtained an Associate Diploma in Engineering in 1997 and achieved several units towards a Graduate Certificate in Management by 2004. Having relocated back to Perth, after 5 years in Melbourne writing strategic papers for his business unit, he settle in Bedford and began writing as hobby.

In 2008, he left the Telecommunications sector and traveled SE Asia, where he finally settled in Cambodia. In 2010, he obtained his TESOL qualifications and a Graduate Diploma in Enterprise Applied Management in 2011. He now teaches English Academic Writing to Khmer ESL students at a well renowned University in Phnom Penh. Stephen is married and enjoys his time with family, teaching, and writing, which are three of his passions. For more information about the author visit Amazon Author Central.

Notes:

1. If you enjoyed or learned something from this book, I would appreciate if you could leave a review on *Amazon*. To Leave a review follow this link, http://www.amazon.com/Academic-Writing-Graduate-Students-Skills-ebook/product-reviews/B00CNBJ6Z4/ref=dp_top_cm_cr_acr_txt?ie=UTF8&showViewpoints=1, for "*Learn English Paragraph Writing Skills*".

2. If you are seeking more information about essay writing techniques then take a look at book II in the series, *Academic Writing Skills*, "*Practical Academic Essay Writing Skills: An International ESL Student Essay Writing Guide*". http://www.amazon.com/Practical-Academic-Essay-Writing-Skills-ebook/dp/B00F1H2G90/ref=sr_1_11?s=digital-text&ie=UTF8&qid=1382087695&sr=1-11&keywords=essay+writing

3. If you are seeking more information about the English essay writing process then take a look at book III in the series, Academic Writing Skills, "The 5 Step Essay Writing Process: English Essay Writing Skills for ESL Students". http://www.amazon.com/Writing-Process--English-Students-Academic-ebook/dp/B00F7J8AGU

4. If you are looking for some practice exercises, try "*English Writing Exercises for International Students: An ESL Grammar*

Workbook for ESL Essay Writing."
http://www.amazon.com/English-Writing-Exercises-International-Students-ebook/dp/B00GPI3CQK . This is an Interactive Workbook written to support all my books in the series *"Academic Writing Skills.*

5. If you wish to follow *Academic Writing Skills*, http://hbicambodia.com/ or be informed of future book releases then *sign up for our reader's newsletter* . http://hbicambodia.com/subscribe-to-aws.html. You can also follow us on Facebook and/or Twitter.

Figure 15 - Author Books in the Series Academic Writing Skills for ESL Students

Stephen E. Dew

TESOL Instructor

Author of the series

Academic Writing Skills

References

- *"Academic Writing for Graduate Students"*,(edition 1). Stephen E. Dew, hbicambodia.com, 2013.
- *"The 5 Step Essay Writing Process"*. Stephen E. Dew, hbicambodia.com, 2013.
- A Journalistic Approach to Good Writing. Robert M. Knight, Wiley, 2003.
- What is Dependent Clause? Wikipedia, 2013.

Resources

I have provided some links to downloadable resources for you to use.

Download the rules for proper nouns

http://db.tt/m7eoTqGV

Download the Detailed Outline example

http://db.tt/QMVmxccW

Download your copy of the peer review checklist

http://db.tt/9aGO4Ilm

Download your copy of the self-edit checklist

http://db.tt/OpP7BPeV

Appendix

Commonly used Transition Signals

Usage	Sentence Connectors	Coordinating Conjunctions	Subordinating Conjunctions	Other
To add another or similar idea	Furthermore,	and		
	Also,	both ... and ...		
	In addition,	not only ... but also ...		
	Finally,			
	Moreover,			
	Similarly,			
	Besides,			
To add an opposite idea or contrast	On the other hand,	but	although	different from
	However,	Yet	even though	differently
			though	unlike
			while	differ from
			whereas	differ in

Usage	Sentence Connectors	Coordinating Conjunctions	Subordinating Conjunctions	Other
To make a comparison	too	and	as	equally
	Also,	both ... and ...	just as	equal to
	Likewise,	not only ... but also ...		the same as
	Similarly,	and ... too		similar to
				just like
To make a contrast	On the other hand,	but	although	different from
	However,	Yet	even though	differently
	In contrast,		though	unlike
			while	differ from
			whereas	differ in

Usage	Sentence Connectors	Coordinating Conjunctions	Subordinating Conjunctions	Other
To give a reason		for	because	Because of + noun
			since	
			as	
To give a result	Therefore,	so		
	Thus,			
	Consequently,			
	As a result,			
To give an example	For example,	but		such as ...
	For instance,	Yet		An example of

Usage	Sentence Connectors	Coordinating Conjunctions	Subordinating Conjunctions	Other
To add a conclusion	All in all,			It is clear that ...
	In brief,			You can see that ...
	Indeed,			These examples show that ...
	In short,			You can see from these examples that ...
	In conclusion,			
	In Summary,			
	To summarize,			
	To conclude,			
	To sum up,			
	For these reasons			

Usage	Sentence Connectors	Coordinating Conjunctions	Subordinating Conjunctions	Other
To list ideas in time order	First,		after	After a while,
	First of all,		as	Before beginning + noun
	Second, etc		as soon as	At last,
	Next,		before	In the evening,
	After that,		since	After ten minutes
	Meanwhile,		until	The next day,
	Finally,		when	Tomorrow,
	then		whenever	The first kind ...
	soon		while	The third step ...
	now			At noon,

Transition between Paragraphs

Sentence Connectors	Subordinators	Prepositions
To add an additional idea		
Furthermore,		Besides + noun ...
In addition,		In addition to ...
Moreover,		
Besides,		
To add an opposing idea		
On the other hand,	Although,	Despite ...
However,	Even though,	In spite of ...

Common transition signals used between paragraphs in essays
to add an additional idea or *to add an opposing idea.*

This Page has been Left BLANK Intentionally

Made in the USA
Columbia, SC
07 December 2017